SOFA SURFIN

Sofa Surfin

Mike Jenkins

Acknowledgements
Roundyhouse; Red Poets; proletarianpoetry.com; Planet; Dream Catcher; 'Martyrs' (Merthyr Town FC programme); culturematters.org.uk.

First published in 2017

© Author: Mike Jenkins
© Gwasg Carreg Gwalch

All rights reserved. No part of this publication may be reproduced, stored in a retrieval system, or transmitted in any form or by any means, electronic, electrostatic, magnetic tape, mechanical, photocopying, recording, or otherwise, without prior permission of the authors of the works herein.

ISBN: 978-1-84527-629-4

Cover design: Eleri Owen
Cover image: Gus Payne

Published with the financial support of the Welsh Books Council.

Published by Gwasg Carreg Gwalch,
12 Iard yr Orsaf, Llanrwst, Wales LL26 0EH
tel: 01492 642031
email: books@carreg-gwalch.com
website: www.carreg-gwalch.com

*Dedicated to John and Helle,
who always had faith in the dialect poems
and with great thanks to Andrew as well.*

Order of poems

Ewsed t be Ooverville	9
Solitree Mister	11
Rose from rubble	12
On'y when I sing	14
I put it there	15
A Lej	16
Ol school	17
No offence!	18
Dogs wanna be	20
A pijin in Greggs	21
African woman at-a markit	22
Excape of-a sand-dog	23
Flip flops in winter	25
Muslims up yer!	26
It's tha Muhammad Ali	27
Pound Shop politics	28
Viagra Falls	30
Merthyr Shark Wrestler	32
Ower town	33
Punished f bein young	34
Starin at-a rain	35
Tha room, a punishment	36
Sofa surfin	37
Fren or pimp	39
The assessment	40
Casualties	41
A practical dance	42
Inta the black	43
Sleepin in-a subway	44
Fly man	45

Sabotage	46
Rubbish sculpture	47
Crawlin on emtee	48
They stopped my benefit	49
Talkin religion	51
Goin somewhere	53
Bruise on er face	54
Tha driver!	55
Guard from north of Ell	56
Im off of X Factor	58
Local celeb	60
Martha the Martyr	61
The Great Excape	62
Las bus ome	63
Inta Spoons	64
Dress-up Dave is back agen	65
The Fightin Season	66
Bard memree	67
One way ticket	69
Int got no balls	70
Outa the undergrowth	71
'Thieves Steal Bridge!'	72
Losin the bus	73
No weather	74
Too bloody weak	75
Where I come from	76

EWSED T BE OOVERVILLE

Em'tiness. Them factree sheds.
The las shift leaves
an ev'ry machine stops.

We ewsed t be Ooverville,
ower washin-machines
sent all over
like rails an cannons
from them ol ironworks.

We could even afford t larf
'bout Sinclair an is C5,
puttin it in-a window
as a crazee failure.

Now, we drive away
f'r the las time
with nowhere t go:
the toy factree's gone
an we ardly make nothin.

It's all retail an ousin
in this once great town:
but oo cun spend
an nobuddy's buildin.

All them yers, all them skills
wasted like my son
with is degree, signin on.

Em'tiness. Rot an rats move in
an on'y the diggers o Ffôs-y-frân
never stoppin like the lines
we left be'ind: the memrees
o frens stay welded,
as joints break an roof's collapsin.

SOLITREE MISTER

Always on is own
ee come from the tips –
never knew is name

as kids we yelled out
'Omo!' an 'Daz!', typical Valleys fashion
like the giant we called Twti –

all is face an ands
woz black as a coal-face
like a creature from underground

ee wore a belt o keys
round is waist, lived in a caravan,
'Ee's a gypo!' sayd my mam

my dad sayd ee'd spend is days
up there scrabblin f'r lumps
sellin them when ee could

is clothes coulda walked off
on theyer own, left im naked –
never yeard im make a sound

once we followed im round town
a gang o shouts, a pack o taunts
an ee give us a glare like a curse

in-a 'Merthyr' they sayd ee'd gone,
some local photographer once caught im –
is ome burnt t the colour of is skin.

ROSE FROM RUBBLE

Ee come yer
with is lens snoopin,
tha photographer.

Im an is reporter butty,
at first we thought
they woz like the rest of em;

feedin off of tragedy –
a good story, grippin picture
an then go away.

But they stayed,
top room of the Mack,
freezing cold, tea at-a chippie.

An when Tom Bunce
(ardes' man in-a village)
wuz gunna pan em out,

they bought im a pint
an we begun t talk
seein they woz tidee.

Ee photoed the kids
oo come out t play,
the first weddin arfta;

showed ow ower lives
adto push on
despite ev'rythin.

Not jest women
standin an waitin
f kids oo never come ome.

Miners, like me, oo'd dug
all night an day
f one cry, one movin limb.

Theyer photos an words
celebratin the survivors –
rose from rubble, dazed an wond'rin.

ON'Y WHEN I SING

I done plenty in my time
an it's not over yet;
went all over with the choir,
fought f'r-a famlees t get
what they deserved.

But it still returns at night,
jest like some soldier
oo carn forget
is butties blown t bits.

Ad my own famlee an kids,
made shewer that they
took ev'ry chance
I never ad, got away
from this Valley, ardly come back.

I wake up sweatin,
I scream in-a middle of sleep,
carn ardly breathe
an-a dead body over me.

Sometimes I wish they woz near,
speshly now my missis ave gone.
The village shops 're closin down
one by one an town's the same,
but I could never leave.

In my nightmare I am there,
it won' leave me move
an nobuddy can yer;
on'y when I sing
the light appears.

I PUT IT THERE

I put it there
(me an other workmen)
an I knew the Coal Board
woz the real criminals,
but I carn elp feelin ...

The tickin of-a stream
below Tip Number 7,
the rain projectin it down'ill
inta a smoke-screen o fog
an then the school.

Feel like I bin workin
f'r the enemy;
Lord Robens an is Boyz
oo shunned responsibility.

In-a days arfta
streets woz emtee
of birdsong an children,
till one by one
they come out t play.

We dug an dug long owers
desperate f any small sounds,
like the sky ud bin
a gallery roof
an ev'ryone caught underground.

A LEJ

Tommy Doc? Yeah, I 'member im,
a lej of the classroom!

Always wore Doc Martens
even though they woz banned.

Long air an never a tie on,
with is posh voice ee tried it on.

Scripts an films, stories an poems,
oo needed borin comprehensions?

On is wall ee painted a muriel
o Dylan Thomas, fag an all.

Tommy Doc come an went like snow,
so fulla dazzle an glow.

Words like snowballs, ower desks
sledges down-slope full pelt.

Ee melted away, jest left,
is walls wuz painted pavement grey.

OL SCHOOL

Aye, them woz the dayz
when teachers wuz teachers
(well, mostly nutters really).

I 'member er like yesterday,
French teacher wern she?
Amazin ow we learnt so much.

She wore a red beret
an always green wellies
wha'ever the weather.

'Bonjour mes animaux!'
she greeted ev'ry class;
strawberry face, ooked nose.

She sometimes wore a surgical mask
speshly in-a winter months
an yew couldn yer er proplee.

She didn take no messin,
if somebuddy farted in er lesson
out come er andy perfume spray.

She woz ol school but ad us
actin scenes from olidays
we'd never get t go on:

orderin wine, lost in Paris,
in a market tastin cheese:
kept er distance, on look-out f disease.

NO OFFENCE!

No offence like,
but yew're a baldy bastard
with an ead like an egg,
if I woz t crack it open
yewer brain ud be
like a Cadbury Cream Egg.

An yewer breath's more mingin
than my dog arfta ee've spewed up,
yew got warts on yewer face
jest like them witches
in ol Shakey's 'Macbeth'.

Ow come yew always sweat
like yew got taps
under yewer armpits:
B.O. = Bog Odour,
ever yeard of deodorant?

Yewer clothes 're so ancient
they'll be back in fashion soon,
yew mus get em from Oxfam;
yewer trainers 're mankin,
yew look like a gypo:
where d'yew live, Bogey Road?

When yew talk it's a bloody screech,
so igh-pitched the dogs go mad
an people in-a shops think
the fire-alarm's gone off,
anybuddy ud think
yew'd ad yewer goolies chopped off!

No offence like!

DOGS WANNA BE

D'yew think dogs
really wanna be
pimped up an preened,
taken f walkies
an dragged away from
walls fulla whiffs?

D'yew think they really
wanna be told when t sit,
shit, eat, lick yewer feet,
jump f'r a treat,
or through burnin oops?

Nah! They wanna be out
with packs of other ounds
discoverin theyer 'inner wolves';
they wanna chase, bonk,
bark, growl an bite,
they wanna sniff bums whenever.

Coz they're a bit like us ewmans,
speshly on oliday
or Saturday in-a city;
apart from-a sniffin bums maybe!

A PIJIN IN GREGGS

This pijin woz struttin is stuff down town,
ee wuz in Greggs lunchtime –
think ee wuz arfta the offer
of 5 ring donuts f'r a pound.

So I sayz to im, I sayz –
'Ow d'yew get in yer, pijin mun?'
'Well', ee replies,' I flew down
from my perch on-a Lucy Thomas Fountain,

then I come up the Igh Street
pas where Anne's Pantree ewsed t be,
pas the New Crown Inn,
the Crown t yew an me… ….

pas where Woolies ewsed t be
tidee sweets in the ol dayz;
pas where Smith's ewsed t be
an-a Body Shop, great f Christmas smellies.

Pas where Dew'urst's ewsed t be,
pickin at-a back, bits o bodies;
pas where-a Co ewsed t be ...
like-a sound 'Co', bit like me.

I come yer f'r a pastie
coz I wanna do a college course
t learn ow t be a seagull
an yeard this is where yew enrol.'

AFRICAN WOMAN AT-A MARKIT

Seen er jest once,
thought I woz seein thin's
(too much medication)
the African woman
servin at-a stall
sellin cheese, bacon an pasties
all embalmed in plastic.

Not like she woz dressed
all bright an colourful
but, sat on er ead
as she served the people,
woz an ewge bag o stuff:
carrots, frewt an thin's,
without a pasty in sight.

All-a time she balanced
tha bag like a footie star
with a ball, so outa place
I wonder now if I dreamt it
on a drab, damp Merthyr day
an nobuddy s much as commented.

EXCAPE OF A SAND-DOG

Ee makes a sand-dog down town
outside of-a Pound Store,
buskin with no sound.

Ee's from Rewmania or summin,
but the dog never stays
an jest when is sculpture is done ...

the retriever up and leaves im
an-a three pups sucklin,
with a long trail be'ind.

Inta the kiddies' nursree
where they all start yelpin
an pattin, it digs in-a sand pit

jest lookin f'r frens
then wanders off to-a buildin site
an neally ends up as concrete!

Outside-a Wyndham this Rottweiler
on a leash is arfta a fight
but the sand–dog shakes grain in its eyes.

A news-ound sniffin out a story
tries t' corner it by a kiosk
(an all-a time it's shrinkin).

Down by-a bus-station the druggies
think they're seein thin's –
'Fuckin ell mun! A dog made o dunes!'

A mangy stray bites off one of its legs
an chokes t death, an it ops
to-a river, 'bout t dive in ...

Vlad the sand-sculptor catches up with it,
scoopin is creation into a bag;
losin its dogginess till-a nex town.

FLIP FLOPS IN WINTER

'Is ee orright or wha?'
the ol lady pointed with er metal stick.

Shorts, t-shirt, flip flops,
tattoos on both arms.

An there's me on a frosty mornin
with a north wind blowin icy,

in my bobble an woolly scarf,
my four layers o thermals;

I'd-a worn a balaclava
on'y I didn wanna be arrested!

'Der, summin wrong with im!'
I agreed, all-a time thinkin:

'Good f r im ... wish I could shed more ...
an jest like me, ee've got no air.'

Seen im in-a Mountain Shop later
searchin f r a bargen in-a ski wear!

MUSLIMS UP YER!

I woz walkin up the ill
(tidee area, real quiet, no trouble)
when I seen em.

Thought I woz bloody allucinatin!
Four of them Muslims –
caps, long white robes an ewge beards.

We don' get nothin
like tha up by yer,
on'y cornershops an doctors.

My first instinct wuz bombs,
oldin ostages, doin be'eadin's;
one carryin a suspicious package.

Sayz t myself – 'Now Dar,
stay calm mun! Reach f'r-a mobile,
no sudden moves or starin.'

'Iya!' one shouts, smilin.
I stares at-a package,
fulla fresh-picked blackberries.

'Orright?' I greeted back.
Maybe buryin summin or a trainin exercise?
Maybe they jest wanted stuff f pies?

IT'S THA MUHAMMAD ALI!

Met im goin down'ill t town,
fit an lean despite the beer,
is ol clothes mingin as is ouse.

We talked 'bout pubs closin down
an some openin, 'bout-a smokin:
as many things as pavin-stones.

'Tha band,' ee sayd, 'from Liverpool,
them with-a guitars ... they started it!'
(ee wuz on 'bout mewsical noise).

As if we woz strollin back in time
t when they'd bin discovered;
but I knew ee'd get there soon ...

'What we need's another war! A big one!
They'll start it, wait an see!
It's all down t tha Muhammad Ali!'

'Yew mean the champion boxer?'
'Nah, im in Iran ... all called Muhammad ...
yew might as well number em!

They'll drop the atom bomb,
they wanna go to eaven, see ...
it's theyer on'y destiny!'

Then ee walks away
inta mewsical noise o the town
ee wuz born, grew up an would die in.

POUND SHOP POLITICS

This bloke see,
ee didn know nothin
bout pol'tics whatsoever.

Nearest ee got to it
woz drinkin in-a Labout Club,
or votin f'r a neighbour oo stood.

If yew arst im
ee'd problee say – 'Labour,
I always vote Labour!'

Ee always ad an eye
f'r a bargen, tha's why
ee loved it in Merthyr.

Charity an Pound shops galore
an ee seen this new one open
down by-a Lucy Thomas Fountain.

It ad a bright purple sign
an a £ clearly displayed.
Ee entered in anticipation.

Expectin loads of is favourite
Belgian chocolates, German beers
an, o course, Italian pasta;

all ee seen wuz a table
fulla leaflets an posters
an a man in a sewt be'ind.

'Wha yew got f'r a quid?' ee arst
an a man showed im two pamphlets:
'No To EU' an 'Cutting Immigration'.

'Got anythin ot as peri-peri
Portuguese sauce like in Nandos?
Or spicy as a tasty chorizo?'

'This is the UKIP shop, my friend,
not another Pound Store.'
Pissed off, ee visited the Polish shop nex door.

VIAGRA FALLS

When yew're thinkin 'bout
the job yew ad in Oovers,
when yew carn get round
even on-a mobility scooter

jest remember –
we're the town
what discovered Viagra

when the on'y fags yew cun get
look like long, thin compewters
an there's no gold left
in–a attic f'r-a pawnbrokers

jest remember –
we invented Viagra

when yewer time down under
stops yew breathin proper,
when yew begin t spend longer
down-a surjree than anywhere

jest remember-
the accidental birthplace o Viagra

when even-a mountains an rivers
don' make yew gasp no longer,
when yew carn make a stand no more
an-a missis calls yew a Droopy Trooper

welcome t Viagra Falls
in ome-town Merthyr!

MERTHYR SHARK WRESTLER

'There's no call f Shark Wrestlers
in this istoric town o Merthyr,'
ee tol me, sighin.

'Look wha I done in Australia,
on-a beach where I give it a welly ...
that shark oo woz a killer!

I woz famous an all, papers an telly;
eero oo fought off a killer fish,
ready t bite the limbs off kiddies.

Merthyr marn, hard as fuck,
don' mess with me, shark but!
till I come ome, that is ...

an lost my bloody job!
I woz on-a sick but I woz recoverin
from depression; we adto get away, see.'

'No call f Shark Wrestlers,' ee tol me
as we queued outside-a laboratree
wonderin which organs ud make mos' money.

OWER TOWN

Ower town is slowly closin down,
one arfta another the shops,
the ouse'old names an local ones,
like old people dyin off
in a neglected Care Ome.

An ev'ryone talkin in
ewsed-t-bes an I remembers
an tha's-where-it-wozs.

Ower town ave moved out
to-a Retail Park no parkin charge,
though we got posh pavin-stones
an a one-way system, straight in an out.

Ower town is closin down
an waitin f'r-a flame an smoke.

PUNISHED F BEIN YOUNG

Whadda bloody ell we done
punished f bein young?

We int goh enough Cs t get on,
we're jest letters t them.

Carn get no jobs see,
the fewture's an emtee ground;

they send us t Charitee shops
an Pound shops t work f nothin.

Gotta live at ome, no choice,
carn afford no flat or ouse.

Yew wonder why we live t fly,
off of ower eads on dope 'n' booze.

Coz bein young's a crime t'day,
always debts an fines t pay.

STARIN AT-A RAIN

Sittin in my wheelchair:
my dad, my carer
elped me there.

My mam's jest lyin
on-a sofa:
some days it its er.

Tampin outside my ome,
no way cun I risk
damp like venom,

like smoke fillin my lungs.
Waitin f'r-a taxi t come,
Council ave promised one.

My dad makes me larf,
ee'll fight my case,
tell em t 'Wise up, or else!'

On'y wanna go t college,
on'y wanna ave a fewture,
despite my anchorin body.

I do get benefits,
yet I'm yer sittin
starin at-a rain.

THA ROOM, A PUNISHMENT

Tha room
tha spare room,
carn afford t decorate no more.

Alive with memrees
of ower kids when young
an still noisy sometimes
when-a gran'children come
fillin it with theyer fun.

Tha room
slike a dungeon,
a cell, a threat,
a debtor's prison.

I'm gonna fight
no matter what –
my appeal flung
on an eap t rot.

Some dayz we go without –
my usban struggling
arfta surgree, pills is food.

Tha room
suddenly a punishment –
gonna stand up to-a Government,
they'll yer me shout!

SOFA SURFIN

Ee've kicked me out
it woz a stewpid argument
'bout a juke-box
'Chirpy Chirpy Cheep Cheep' –
I fuckin sayd 'No way!'
(shame no Beef'eart).

Ee've kicked me out
without even a key
t get all I owned,
a sleepin-bag; my phone
woz dead as my life become.

Ee wuz the final one.
Ever tried it mun?
Ever tried balancin
on a fuckin sofa
when yewer ands shake
like it's always winter?

Ever tried ridin the waves
of forms an offices,
find an answer in impossible paper?
Ever tried goin under,
I mean drownin alive
below all yewer memrees?

Coz I'm talkin 'bout the breakers
ewger than any sea's –
divorce an booze, gettin sacked an speed.
Ow I stood on-a board
f moments before bein dragged down
t the subway, like an underwater tunnel
where I could ardly breathe.

FREN OR PIMP?

Woz ee my fren or my pimp?
Did ee give me is key
jest coz we woz partners in drink?

Ee give me is kitchen, is sofa.
Ee wan'ed money f ev'rythin,
even the water I drunk.

I woz the thief locked in
t the ouse I wuz burglin
an ee woz the jailer.

Is cans wen' missin,
always me not the others,
oo come arfta pills an dope.

Tried t set me up with this woman,
er usban' a soldier he sayd
(I reckon ee'd gone down).

'Yew'll make good money outa it.
All's yew gotta do is fuck er.
Er usban' won' know a thing.'

Woz ee my fren or my pimp?
I owe im loads, I owe im nothin.
Ad a key t my own prison.

THE ASSESSMENT

I crawled inta the Assessment
arfta my ESA,
I ad a walkin stick
my ands all gnarled
my ips killin me,
an the Depression tabs
playin ell with my ead
makin me a zombie.

They stared at me
like I wuz tellin lies,
like I woz a cheatin fraud;
it woz interrogation
tha's fit f spies.

If on'y 'ey could see my pain
an the darkness show up
in an X-ray of my brain
an ev'ry bone an vein
light up like neon
to expose my suff'rin.

Waitin f the appeal,
waitin on death row
f money t save me
or fuckall t finish me –
volts through my body.

CASUALTIES

Yew cun build a bridge over-a river
f'r-a road t go past the bran' new college,
but the on'y way this town
is travellin is down.

They jumped from the footpath under,
place where the druggies go
t pump theirselves full
b'fore they lose ev'rythin.

Most problee they woz outa
theyer skulls when they decided
t fly t'gether without wings;
crazee canaries in-a daylight.

To most they woz jest names,
more casualties in an unnamed war,
bleedin from wounds inside;
cept I wen' t school with er.

I 'member when er mother died
an ow she couldn cope no more,
er ol man spectin er t be suddenly old;
but she wuz 14, bright in class, didn care.

Them yers I woz learnin a trade
she lost er feathers one by one;
the week b'fore I seen er in town:
she woz skinny as a skellington.

A PRACTICAL DANCE

I woz doin this dance
it woz a practical dance
I left nothin t chance

I woz on my own
as the band played loud
Local Enemy at-a Club

it woz aimed at im
it woz timed f Securitee
woz opin ee'd ave a pop at me

I woz doin this dance
an there wuz no romance
it woz a purposeful dance

ee wuz like a toad on speed
or a frog on coke
or a skunk on skunk

ee'd groped my young fren
in a nearby pub
an ee wuz at it agen

so I woz doin this dance
it woz a practical dance ...
but ee never ad a go at me.

INTA THE BLACK

I dropped off of yewer system,
don' afto sign on,
I int no statistic
an yew carn stop my benefit
coz my missis got a job
an I'm sick o disappointment.

There's over a million
jest like me,
fallen off of the edge
of compewter cliffs
an inta the black,
landed on a ledge.

I like it down yer
idin in-a dark,
there's plenty o sharks
like ev'rywhere else,
but least I int chasin
along pointless paths.

Yew carn see me now
or send snoopers down,
rocks below are perilous
as men o war;
an I'm like a goat
clamberin an leapin over laws.

SLEEPIN IN-A SUBWAY

Down inta the subway
call it ell, call it Ades,
I take my place
with the rollin cans
an piles o waste.

If on'y I ad rats
f companee or mangy strays;
ee've flung me out, no key.
Concrete bed, the flat above
got motors an wheels.

Wearin my blankets
jacket an jumper,
I keep expectin visitors,
some gang o piss-eads
ewsin me as a target.

No spice or skunk
t carry all my worries
far from my shiverin body.
I curl inta a foetus,
wish I woz a baby.

FLY MAN

I chose t take the rough path,
the one the people ad trod
not the smooth tarmac.

There woz broken glass underfoot
an I wuz dressed all in black,
carryin a bucket o paste f postin.

Soon as I spotted the cops
I blended inta the night
up the gwli, no panic.

Brush in my ands wuz sticky.
I'm a flyboy, don' need no wings,
they int gonna swat me!

Ev'ry cause I put up
over the yers from anti-poll tax
t calls f'r a Welsh Republic.

I know all-a bes places,
most of em I've pissed on
late night an off of my face.

There's more now 'an ever ewsed t be,
all-a closed down buildins an shops.
I'm a Fly Man ... nobuddy gonna catch me!

SABOTAGE

I ewsed t work with video machines
up Irwin, till ey closed
tha factree down.

An then, on-a lines
makin desks an filin cabinets
some robots coulda done.

I lost ev'rythin arfta:
wife, job an ome;
darkness like no other.

At las I'm comin up agen,
startin t breathe pewer air:
there's a new factree openin.

I don' wanna do it.
makin armoured cars
f fewture bloody wars.

I marched the streets b'fore
'gainst Iraq, Afghanistan an Gaza.
I don' take it, my benefit disappears.

Orready I'm plannin t scheme:
a wire yer, a loose connection.
Sabotage, s nobuddy knows.

RUBBISH SCULPTURE

I picked em up
on-a way t nowhere in p'ticlar
and now this is becomin
my rubbish sculpture.

It's arf creature, arf machine
an arf ewman:
tha's three arves
coz it's bigger 'an one.

There's a bike chain,
a doll's leg, purple scarf
an an ol syringe,
wheel ub an cushion spring –

there's a fisherman's float,
collar off of a dog,
a rusty door-knob
an two CND yer-rings.

It int finished by no means,
I'm buildin it up,
I'm twistin an bindin
till I find its name –

till it leaps or crawls
from my flat, down the ill
inta town, all-a waste
suddenly matterin agen.

CRAWLIN ON EM'TEE

Now I know wha-a Big Society is really,
it's like a ewge ole in-a stomachs
of my small famlee.

My two kids, Jade an Shania,
I carn afford t feed em no more,
school olidays 're worse 'an ever.

I tried f'r jobs, got big ideas,
but arf a time don' even yer:
slike droppin paper down a disewsed mine.

My mam as t work, my dad's on sick;
las thing I want is charitee,
but the Food Bank ave saved me.

'Mam, I'm starvin! Wha's f' tea?'
Beans, beans an more beans;
all yew yer on telly's 'bout obesity.

Shania an Jade are dead scrawny,
there's a big ole in theyer lives,
theyr crawlin, not runnin, on em'tee.

THEY STOPPED MY BENEFIT

They stopped my benefit
an what ave I got
left in-a flat?
Two boggin tea-bags
an a tin o sardines
outa date!

Say I never
signed on, but
I know theyer
system's t blame;
it's appened before
'Fuck off!' a-compewter sayz.

I always woz a worker
ever since sixteen:
in factrees
I ad skills
an now I'm a nothin,
too ol f'r ev'ry job.

Lucky my landlor'
is a tidee bloke,
lucky I get adopted
in pubs by frens
buy me booze
take me with em.

Oo wan's somebuddy
cun draw cartoons,
cun tell yew anythin
'bout folk, rock an blues?

They stopped my benefit
but carn stop my life:
gimme a pencil an a pint,
juke-box playin Neil Young,
jest gimme a book
an my ead'll be buzzin!

TALKIN RELIGION

Mormuns in pairs
an Jovies in gangs –
I love talkin to em
better 're any politicians.

With them Mormuns I d' say –
'Ow many wives yew got?
I'm livin with my missis
but we int married.
Wan a cuppa tea?
I need one coz I woz pissed
outa my ead las night.
Bin drinkin too much,
started seein thin's,
angels an stuff …
but yew'd understand.'

With-a Jovies I d' say –
'My son's in ospital
ad to ave a blood transfusion,
yew'd let im die though.
When's-a world gunnew end,
nex week, month, year?
On'y yew gunnew be saved,
not the likes o me
one o Satan's boyz!
By the way, it's my birthday
wan a piece o cake
an a cup o coffee?'

Mormuns on theyer mission
an Jovies sellin 'Watch Tower' –
they stand open-mouthed an lissen,
then rapidly do a runner.

GOIN SOMEWHERE
For Gemma June Howell

It's winter an I'm goin somewhere.
Carn sit down
my ead's buzzin.

I'm on evr'ythin,
givin my number
an dealin a quick one.

I'm up an down
like a restless prick,
I'm a gobby cow, mouthy bitch.

Don' take no messin.
See-a tattoo of a snake
on my shoulder blade?

Well, tha's gunna jump
an bite any bastard
tries t fuck me about.

It's winter an I wear a black vest,
my blonde-dyed air the colour
of a manky sheep.

Don' follow nobuddy,
no dog's gonna round me up.
Goin somewhere, but it int on-a map.

BRUISE ON ER FACE

When she got on-a bus
we woz all so shocked;
seen straight away
the bruise on er face
like a map of a countree
all blackened by blood.

'D'yew fall over?' somebuddy asks,
she jest shook er ead
an never answered.

But I knew im,
knew what ee wuz like,
my Ken tol me
arfta too many beers
ow ee could turn.

'I've never done nothin
t deserve this!' she wailed.
I eld er and
as others sayd 'Take care!'

'People got nothin but good
t say about yew, Kay!'
Could ardly look at er face
all swollen with pain,
er eyes puffed up,
the bags they carried
eavier day by day.

THA DRIVER!

Im! Im b'there! Tha driver!

Im with-a graveyard teeth
an a bloody cackle
like-a witches off of Shakespeare.

Ee took us t Daffodils ee did
an not inta town,
thinks ee's funny ee does,
a proper clown.

Jest coz we all got bus passes,
ee's always goin on 'bout ower ages.

Took us t the Ol Folks Ome,
stopped outside an sayd –
'Right yew lot! Get off yer
coz none of yew's paid!'

Yeah, im b'there!
Im elpin with-a trolleys an push-chairs.
Thinks ee cun get away with it
jest coz ee knows ev'ryone.

Well, ee don' know my name!

GUARD FROM NORTH OF ELL

See im comin
down the aisle
beard an beer-gut
six foot three,
with is expression
like a Monday mornin,
ee's-a guard
from north of Ell.

Carn ewse yewer railcard
shoulda ewsed the machine
that wern workin;
yew under sixteen
oo yew kiddin?

I 'member this one bloke
sleepin arfta work feet up
an ee knocks em flyin
'What the fuck?'
this bloke swung without thinkin.
The guard threatens t fling im
off-a train next stop;
come Merthyr the p'lice
woz on board
but, fair play, let im off.

See im comin down the aisle
voice like a moany Ead
sniffin out booze an vapes,
pushin is beer-gut
inta the faces o school kids
igh on the end o the week.

The guard from Quakin Yard
is ome village –
don' try it on,
ee's there even if ee int,
got eyes on-a ceilin.

IM OFF OF X-FACTOR

It fuckin woz,
I seen im!

                    On ower street?

Yeah, Ben Barzoni!

                    Wha, im off of X-Factor,
                    the runner-up?

Yeah, ee wuz walkin
towards the Red
with a whool gang,
oldin an acoustic guitar.
Ee looked bigger
than on-a telly
an older ... well ...
ee is by now anyway.

                    D'yew get it ...
                    y'know ... is autograph?

Nah, too busy messin
with my mobile,
ended up takin a photo
of my feet.

                    Did ee play the guitar?

I dunno, I on'y
seen is back.

                    Well, ow d'yew know
                    f shewer it woz im?

Coz I shouts out –
'Ey Ben, wha's appnin?'
an ee never turns round.

                                        Well, tha proves it 'en!

LOCAL CELEB

Ewsed t know im see,
before ee become a celebritee.
People say it's jest jealousy.

We both done Drama in school
so ow come I'm the one
signin up on the dole,

while ee's in tha Soap?
'Fame's a bubble cun pop!'
I kid myself when I see im.

'Orright Jase?' ee sayz t me
'wanna drink?' but I int takin
nothin off of is charitee.

All them mates ee've got
an girlz all over im,
s'obvious what they wan'.

Ee come over like some ironmaster's son,
some Crawshay: ev'ry girl is maid,
ev'ry boy is servant ...'cept one.

MARTHA THE MARTYR

Let me tell yew
Martha the Martyr's in onour
of no ordinree zebra.

It int the crossin
down by Caedraw flats,
or any other f' that matter.

It's coz of an excaped one
back when-a Martyrs begun
before even I woz born.

Coz yew're my gran'son
I'm tellin yew this, see,
it's all part of ower istree.

Got out of a circus,
wen' on the run,
ended up in Pen'darren.

Somebuddy seen it grazin
on a football field:
thought they wuz dreamin!

So if yew think it's weird
tha Merthyr got a zebra f'r a mascot,
instead of a squirrel or pijin,

jest remember tha first one
the original Martha,
not a striped donkey, but genuine.

THE GREAT EXCAPE

My mam lives in an Ome
down by where The Great Excape ewsed t be.

One day she wen wan'drin
an searchin f Steve McQueen.

She wen inta the buildin
an arst f'r a G an T.

They woz kind an elpful,
the men from-a fewnral parlour.

I live not far away from er,
jest up the ill;

an sometimes my own memree
slike pot-oles in-a street.

My dad ewsed t ride a motorbike
jest like Steve McQueen.

Years ago they pulled down-a sign,
but never put up a coffin.

LAS BUS OME

Wagons roll, drive!
Wagons roll!'

It's-a las bus ome:
cans poppin,
couples in wrestlin olds,
man out of it an snorin,
others jokin on theyer phones.

Strong smell from-a back,
a cloud o perfumed smoke
driftin down the aisle
an the driver starts t larf
all on is own accord.

As if we're floatin
up the A470,
up in-a clouds
over Aberfan an Troedyrhiw
jest like them ang-gliders.

It's-a las bus ome
an lucky nobuddy's on-a roads
coz-a driver's got this grin
like an Allowe'en mask,
is mind's a candle flick'rin.

INTA SPOONS

We wen inta Spoons down town,
coupla pints before-a serious stuff.

We wuz larfin 'bout-a news
an all-a jokes on Facebook.

The menu seemed so ordinree
arfta David Cameron's uni club.

'Bloody ell, not much yer!' sayz Lee,
'maybe the cannelloni ud fit!'

'Ow bout them onion rings?'
'Nah, they're bound t sting.'

So I go t the bar to order.
'Table number?' she sayz. '69.'

An tha's when I go mad –
'Got a pig's ead I cun shag?

Followed by a fat juicy melon ...
my butty's more a frewt marn.'

Tha's when she called-a manager,
oo give me a final warnin.

'Bloody ell mun, this int fair,
if it's good enough f'r-a Prime Minister ...'

DRESS-UP DAVE IS BACK AGEN

Bloody ell, I seen im!
I seen im down town agen,
Dress-up Dave bin away frages
an ee wuz wearin a crown.

In-a Works lookin at cheapo books;
not jest any ol crown
but a tidee We Three Kings one,
though ee ad is sewt on.

Almos sif ee wuz gettin back
to is ol ways arfta time
underground or in Outer Space;
or per'aps an institution.

Not even a placard sayin
'Balthazar Dave' angin,
but with all the glam an glitz
on is fancy ead-gear.

I seen im, Dress-up Dave,
ordinree up to is fore'ead
an then, a nest o jewels.
All ail King o the Presink!

THE FIGHTIN SEASON

Black Friday, Black Saturday, the fightin season.
An always comin inta Merthyr Vale station
it begins real serious an crazee.

Drunken drongos or piss'ead footie fans,
yew jest know it's gunna kick off
before Securitee cun move in.

Or, there's no uniforms, an this woman
gets between em, so one calls er 'Slag!'
She's braver than any man.

There's fuckin this an fuckin tha
an bloody bastard shittin,
there's fists an feet an gobbin.

Like-a train's bin eld t ransom
an us kidnapped on-a platform.
An-a p'lice? They miss ev'rythin!

BARD MEMREE

Seen im at-a ground,
the Merthyr speed king.

I knew im well
from the ol Soul Crew dayz.

Now I got a famlee, settled down,
take my son to-a games.

Twice ee've bin sent down,
drugs and GBH I bleeve.

'Wha's appnin but!' ee sayz
jest like we wuz young agen.

Could see is eyes wide
an glarin; ee wuz on pins.

We shared stories of firms
and Feds, always the fightin.

'Member when he got taken in
f settin fire to-a Union Jack in-a Den.

On-a train back ome, in Cardiff
I yeard it kickin off.

Im alone takin on Ipswich fans
an securitee flung im off.

On-a platform, surrounded by cops;
bard memree, as we left im be'ind.

ONE WAY TICKET

'Know yew always wan'ed t travel,' she sayz,
'an ow yew always d' say
we on'y ever go t Tenby,
an if we're lucky Cardigan Bay.'

'Well,' she sayz with a loud smile,
'I booked yew an oliday
of a lifetime, summin special,
it'll be totelee unforgettable!'

I could ardly contain myself,
what a 60th birthday presen', eh?
Would it be the Caribbean
or maybe the sights o Rome?

'I carn come with yew sadly,' she explained,
'it'll on'y be f'r one.'
'C'mon love, urry up an tell me ...
Beaches? City break? Cruisin?'

'Well, yew gotta go really far.'
'Australia? Canada? New Zealand?'
'No, I booked yew a one way ticket
to the lovely planet o Mars.'

INT GOT NO BALLS!

Women in rock
is like chess in pubs,
or rugby without goin
on-a piss before'and.

Women do b'long in-a crowd
or angin 'bout backstage.
When it comes t playin
they should stick t folk,

or teeny-bop stuff
or soul ballads, dressed up:
a Gemma Page in Led Zep,
cun yew imagine tha?

Le's face it, women
int got no balls!
Rock's a mewsical boxin bout:
they cun scream, but carn shout.

OUTA THE UNDERGROWTH

Outa the undergrowth by B an Q's they come
off of theyer eads on cheapo rocket fuel.

It's a glorious Mediterranean day in Merthyr,
ev'ryone's wearin socks 'n' shorts 'n' trainers.

Towards the church, clutchin plastic bottles
they're screamin an yellin, larfin an barkin.

A woman crosses over an I slow down;
seen em before but I'm still on pins.

They're flingin stones at lamp-posts
in some crazee competition.

The pavement's a tight-rope
an they keep on fallin.

The woman's eyes like a bird
with a cat close by, stalkin.

They ewse fewnral cones as loud-ailers,
callin on-a dead t answer.

'THIEVES STEAL BRIDGE!'

Outside-a newsagents I seen the eadlines
'THIEVES STEAL BRIDGE!!!'
sif this town wuz livin up
to its repewtation.

I thought o the Missis
on the way ome down-a A470
an would she disappear
inta a chasm by Pentrebach?

Thought o my son goin swimmin
down Rhydycar an would ee
afto swim the river
jest t get t the Leisure Centre?

An my dad walkin is dog,
would ee think of it
as an ewge gap in is brain,
that ee wuz gettin dementia?

Thought of ones over main roads,
them A-shaped structures
don' seem t be going nowhere;
nobuddy'd notice if they woz missin.

For once I bought the 'Merthyr'
an they adn stole the whool thing,
jest loadsa iron bars!
Still, it got me thinkin.

LOSIN THE BUS

My mam is late
an there's me waitin
f'r er t baby-sit.

Bein a single mam
I ardly ever get out.
Night on-a piss with-a girlz.

Kayleigh's playin up
doin my ead in,
question arfta question.

Mam never replies t texts,
er phone's like summin
outa Cyfarthfa Museum!

Finelee she's yer an Kayleigh
is all over er ... I'm nothin.
'Mam, where yew bin?'

'I lost the bus, din I?'
'Ow cun yew lose a bus?'
'No love, I jest lost it.'

Didn make no sense
till I remembered Welsh lessons
an-a word 'colli'.

'Oh, I got it ... colli bws.'
Looked at me like I got two eads –
'What yew on? Yew off 'en?'

NO WEATHER

We aven ad no weather this summer,
it's bin rain, rain an more rain.

Where's the bus? I complained
t the Council, they sayd it woz on'y me.

Bin t Marks yet? Food All's brilliant,
but the whool town's run down.

What appened in Paris wuz beyond!
It's all them refugees, see …

it's bound t be, they come over yer
but arf o them are gee-addies.

An tha woman welcomin them in Germany,
yew think they'd won the war!

Personally, I carn stand the Germans.
No sign of-a bus. There's snow on-a way.

TOO BLOODY WEAK

We carn do it, see.
there's no way
we'd survive on ower own.

We're too bloody weak –
all tha money
come from Brussels an now London.

Ow we gonna live
off of real ale, whisky,
cheese, veg an milk?

I know we got water
but oo's gunna buy it, Liverpool?
It int exactly oil!

We don' produce nothin
on'y wind, food an poetree
an oo cun live off of these?

Slike we're buskin, see,
playin the same ol tewns,
desperate f a few coins.

They see us an pass by –
'Well they are doing something,
but it's not proper really!'

WHERE I COME FROM

Where I grew up, Plane Grove.
When I woz a kid
I thought it woz great,
all them other streets
named arfta trees an plants –
Marigold, Acacia an Oak,
but owers an aeroplane.

None of us seen many trees
or bushes or flowers –
no gardens ardly
jest loadsa grass
f'r-a dogs t shit on.

Where I come from, the Gurnos,
course we all take drugs,
get pissed all-a time,
think we're fuckin ard,
we all do time, get fat
an moan 'bout immigrants
takin work we don' want –
'cept I got out
wen t college, got a tidee job.

It's better now f definite,
murals an not graffiti,
glass an not bricked up –
an the plane's a tree
growin rapid t shelter and shield,
standin ewge an proud
like my parents ewsed t be.